Be an eco hero

At School

By Sue Barraclough
Photography by Chris Fairclough

W

FRANKLIN WATTS
LONDON • SYDNEY

This edition 2012

Franklin Watts
338 Euston Road
London NW1 3BH

Franklin Watts Australia
Level 17/207 Kent Street
Sydney, NSW 2000

Series editor: Sarah Peutrill
Art director: Jonathan Hair
Design: Big Blu Design
Illustration: Gary Swift
Photography: Chris Fairclough, unless otherwise credited

Credits: Ian Bracegirdle/istockphoto: 8. Westphalia/istockphoto:
16c. A. Wrangler/istockphoto: 13tr. Every attempt has been
made to clear copyright. Should there be any inadvertent
omission please apply to the publisher for rectification.

Many thanks to the children and teachers of Ashton Gate
Primary School, Bristol for their eco-ideas and help and for taking
part in the photo shoot.

Dewey number: 371

ISBN 978 1 4451 0717 2

Printed in China

Franklin Watts is a division of Hachette Children's Books,
an Hachette UK company.
www.hachette.co.uk

Contents

Find out ways to help your planet in this book and become an eco hero like me!

Words in **bold** are in the glossary on page 28.

At school

Schools are busy places. Schools are full of people working and learning. **Energy** is used to light and heat the school and to make machines such as computers work.

Schools use lots of water and **materials** such as paper. Schools also make lots of **rubbish.**

Water

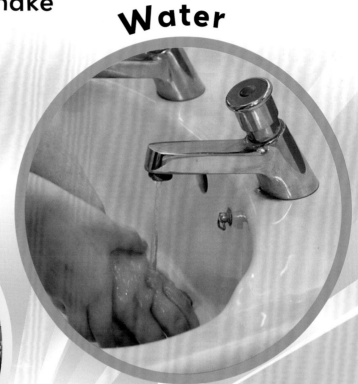

Paper

Rubbish

Using less energy

Most energy comes from burning **fossil fuels**. Finding and using fossil fuels also makes dangerous gases that are causing **climate change**. Fossil fuels will not last forever and we are using them up fast.

Be an eco hero by:

- Switching off lights in empty rooms to save energy.
- Switching off computers and other machines when you have finished with them.
- Closing doors and windows to save heat in cold weather.

This school has eco **monitors** who check classrooms and make sure everyone remembers to switch off the lights.

Using less water

We need water to drink to stay alive. We use water for washbasins and toilets. We use water for growing plants and for washing and cleaning. Clean, fresh water is **precious**.

Eco heroes do not waste water.

Be an eco hero by:

- Telling a teacher about dripping taps.

- Having taps that turn off automatically.

SAVE WATER

- Having water-saving devices in toilets.

Busy roads

Children and teachers need to travel to and from school almost every day. If everyone goes to school by car, this makes the roads very busy.

Busy roads are bad because:

- Cars make dangerous gases that pollute the air.

- **Pollution** can damage your health.

- Roads are dangerous and difficult to cross.

Keeping engines going while parked is especially polluting!

13

Cut down pollution

There are easy ways to cut down pollution and traffic on the roads.

Be an eco hero by:

- Sharing lifts in the car.

- Walking or cycling instead of going by car.

- Helping to set up a **walking bus.**

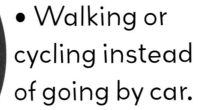

If a school has plenty of bike racks, children are more likely to use bikes or scooters to get to school.

Walking, cycling or scooting to school gets your brain working! It also helps to keep your body fit and healthy.

Rubbish problems

We are using up materials fast, so we need to use them more carefully. It is important not to **waste** materials and to throw less rubbish in the bin. Most rubbish is buried in huge holes called **landfill sites**.

We are running out of space to bury rubbish. So we need to **reduce**, **reuse** and **recycle** our rubbish. If every person in every school uses less it can make a big difference.

This school has small containers for recycling food and garden waste.

Eco heroes help to recycle rubbish!

Reducing rubbish

Every day, we all make lots of rubbish. We throw away packets, cartons, yogurt pots, wrappers and leftover food.

Be an eco hero by:

- Using a refillable drinks bottle.
- Using a lunchbox with sections so you do not need to wrap food.
- Choosing **recyclable** materials such as foil if you do wrap foods.
- Choosing foods with less **packaging.**

If food waste is sent to a landfill site, it breaks down without enough air. This makes dangerous gases that are a cause of climate change.

This food waste will be taken away and made into compost.

Reusing things

If you reuse something you make the best use of the time, money, energy and materials used to make it.

This greenhouse is made from plastic bottles!

• Using both sides of every piece of paper.

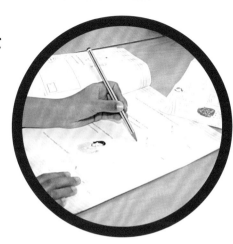

• Reusing packaging, such as yogurt pots and tin cans, for crafts and gardening.

What ways can you think of to reuse everyday objects?

Recycling materials

Food, paper, glass, metal and some plastics can be recycled. It is important to sort different materials as they are more likely to be recycled.

Paper

You can be an eco hero by sorting materials for recycling. Put materials in the right bin or container. Read the signs so you know which bin to use.

Put fruit waste in the right bin so it can be recycled.

Eco heroes sort out materials for recycling!

Green and growing

You can be an eco hero by growing your own vegetables at school. Growing plants is fun to do and you will have fresh, healthy food to eat.

Pull out weeds so plants grow well.

A school garden is good because:

- You learn how to grow fresh food to eat.
- It helps wildlife such as bees and butterflies.
- You can sell plants and **produce** to raise money for other eco projects.

New potatoes

Fresh produce

Salad

Eco hero activities

Reduce
Reuse
Recycle!

Here are some ways you can be creative to be an eco hero at school.

Take part in a **campaign** to change something you don't like. You can pin up posters, hand out leaflets or write emails.

Get crafty! Make
a birdfeeder from
reused materials
and hang it up in a
tree at school.

Hold a 'swap shop'.
Ask everyone to bring
small toys and books or
magazines to swap at school.
The only rule is that if you can't swap
it, you must take it home again!

Glossary

campaign   speak out and take action to change things.

climate change   harmful changes to our planet and weather caused by pollution.

energy   something that makes things work, move or change.

fossil fuel   materials, such as oil, coal and natural gas, found deep under the ground that formed millions of years ago from dead animals and plants.

landfill site   a hole in the ground where rubbish is buried.

material   substance that is used to make things.

monitor   someone who checks if things are done.

packaging   bottles, packets and boxes used to keep food and other products safe and fresh.

pollution   substance that dirties or poisons air, earth or water.

precious   something that has great value because it is rare, expensive or important.

produce   food that is grown to be sold.

recyclable   something made of materials that can be recycled.

recycle   to turn a used material into something new.

reduce   to make less.

reuse   to use something again.

rubbish   things that you throw away that you no longer need or want.

walking bus   a group of adults and children that walk to school together.

waste   use too much of something especially when there is not very much of it.

Learn more

This book shows you some of the ways you can be an eco hero. But there is plenty more you can do at school to save the planet. Here are some websites where you can learn more:

www.walktoschool.org.uk
Meet Strider, the National Walk to School mascot. Also has lots of facts, games and stories.

www.iwalktoschool.org
Find out more about why walking to school is a good idea.

www.recyclezone.org.uk
Visit the different zones to find out about reducing, reusing and recycling your rubbish.

www.recycle-more.co.uk
Click on 'schools' to find out about awards and activities.

www.foe.org.uk
Click on 'learning' to find out more about 'Green up your school' and other campaigns.

www.rspb.org.uk/youth/learn/index.asp
Find out about the Big Schools' Birdwatch, wildlife awards and much more.

Note to parents and teachers: Every effort has been made by the Publishers to ensure that these websites are suitable for children, that they are of the highest educational value, and that they contain no inappropriate or offensive material. However, because of the nature of the Internet, it is impossible to guarantee that the contents of these sites will not be altered. We strongly advise that Internet access is supervised by a responsible adult.

Index